■ Places/Everyone

The Brittingham Prize in Poetry

The University of Wisconsin Press Poetry Series

Ronald Wallace, General Editor

Jim Daniels **Places/Everyone**

The University of Wisconsin Press

Published 1985

The University of Wisconsin Press
114 North Murray Street
Madison, Wisconsin 53715

The University of Wisconsin Press, Ltd.
1 Gower Street
London WC1E 6HA, England

Printings 1985, 1986

Printed in the United States of America

Library of Congress Cataloging-in-Publication Data
Daniels, Jim.
  Places/everyone.
  (The Brittingham prize in poetry ; 1)
  I. Labor and laboring classes—Michigan—
Detroit—Poetry. I. Title. II. Series
PS3554.A5635P5   1985   811'.54   85-40366
ISBN 0-299-10350-1
ISBN 0-299-10354-4 (pbk.)

dedicated to my grandfather, Raymond A. Daniels,

my parents, Raymond J. and Mary T. Daniels,

my sister, Kathleen, and my brothers, Mike, Dave, and Tim

Contents

Foreword

"Many indispensible truths, which could save men, go unspoken for reasons of this kind; those who could utter them cannot formulate them and those who could formulate them cannot utter them. If politics were taken seriously, finding a remedy for this would be one of its more urgent problems."

Thus Simone Weil, who had herself put in a time of brutal and exhausting work on an assembly line, and who made the experience an integral part of her spiritual philosophy, defined the central issue which Jim Daniels has confronted in his poetry. We don't really know from Daniels' work what his own experiences have been in the world of American labor. Clearly they are extensive, but Daniels' project is not to convince us of the legitimacy and authenticity of his own life. His is a poetry of persona, of imaginative sympathy and sophisticated humility. His character Digger labors mythically, and suffers heroically from a system which continues to demand of its worker the consciousness of a machine and the soul of a medieval peasant.

There is a tradition, however marginal, of a sort of proletariat poetry in American literature. Most of it dates from the early part of this century, before labor had been co-opted by various Red scares of its radical awareness and hope, and from the thirties, when economic crisis brought that awareness to the surface again, only to be distracted from it again by the Second World War and McCarthyism.

In the age of Reagan the issues of labor and its manipulation have been, if possible, even more obfuscated and confused. Recession and a consciously willed deficit now have become a means for the reactionary repeal of social progress, and the worker's consciousness, under the pressure of relentless economic insecurity, has become ever more amputated and almost classically depressed. The political helplessness and despair which should be a part of political discourse and discussion, but which are not, are driven instead into the body and the soul, and that soul reacts with tragic and harried spinnings on itself, in its sorrowful intuition that life does not have to be lived this way, no matter how deceived we are into believing that it must be.

These are the subjects and the themes and the unspoken tensions of Jim Daniels' remarkable poetry. He has captured and enacted the blind and sad anguish of souls so trapped that they have ceased to know how to speak even to themselves, but he has never lost sight of the remarkable dignity, humor, and spiritual resilience which at the end are what redeems our passion and our hope. It is our great fortune that Daniels has, in Weil's terms, both formulated and uttered.

C. K. Williams
Brittingham Prize Judge for 1985

ONE

My Grandfather's Tools

Lifetime tinkerer, fixer upper
always with his shiny tools
in his basement, his workbench
scarred wood blessed with oil
an altar to patience and a steady hand.

My grandfather, the unpaid Mr. Fixit
for the church across the street
and their rectory, convent, school.
My grandfather, no true believer
hedges bets with his tools.

He worked for Packard nearly fifty years,
all his life his joy
that feel of tool in hand—
his knife, his gun, his fistful of bills—
showing the engineers how things
really worked.

His old Packard still runs
despite all logic—
his eternal child
as long as he can get the parts.

Over eighty years, still greasing
his hands under the hood of a car,
black magic balm under his nails,
still a firm grip on the tools.

■

My grandfather sleeps in his front room
while I pound on the door
a radio apart on the floor

alone with his tools
the reflection of steel.

He replaces a casting in the steering column
and loses reverse gear.
He charges tools on his credit card,
forgets, my father pays the bills.

The logic of dying escapes him,
no wrench or screwdriver to save
his thinning body. I smell death
in his hands: already dirt is gone
from under his nails.

When he dies, we'll all file down
into his basement to sort tools hanging
from hooks, filling drawers, shelves, toolboxes,
and we'll hold them in our hands, feel their weight,
pallbearers carrying off those clean bones,
no one there to carve them back
into tools.

My Father Worked Late

Some nights we were still awake
my brother and I, our faces smearing the window
watching the headlights bounce up the driveway
like wild pitches of light
thrown by a tired moon.
We breathed in the huge silence
after the engine died
then ran to the door, grabbing his legs
as if we could hold him there
through night, morning, forever.

Some nights when he wasn't too tired
he took off his shirt
and sat in the middle of the floor.
We wrestled, trying to pin
back his arms, sitting on his chest
digging our heads into the yellow stains
under the arms of his t-shirt.
Each time we thought we had him
Do you give, huh, do you give?
he sat up, cradling us both in headlocks
in the closest thing to an embrace
that I remember, and carried us to bed.

Other nights he looked right through us
mechanically eating his late dinner
yelling at anything that moved.
Some mornings we woke to find him
asleep on the couch, his foreman's tie twisted
into words we couldn't spell.
We ate our cereal as carefully as communion
until our mother shook him ready for another day.

■

My father carries no wallet full of lost years
carries no stubs, no guarantees, no promises.
We could drive toward each other all night
and never cross the distance of those missing years.

Today, home for a visit,
I pull in front of the house.
My father walks down the steps
limping from his stroke
he is coming toward me
both of us pinned to the wind
he is looking at me as if to say
give, give, I give,
as if either of us
had anything left to give.

My Mother Walks

She writes letters full of bowling scores
and prayers, covering
what takes her out each night
on flat, familiar streets.

My father reads the paper
scans the tv guide with vague hope.
He tells her she'll kill herself
that it's too hot or too cold

too dangerous, too crazy
but each night she pulls on
what she needs and steps out
the door: one foot, the other.

She walks past the crippled cars
which line these streets, past
the barking dogs, the whiff
of a late barbecue

past the silence of streetlights,
the passive trees, angry bushes,
past the names of her children
faded in cement, counting the miles

the times she's wanted to leave, walks
away from the box with her name on it,
walks until she's afraid enough
to turn around.

Wheels

My brother kept
in a frame on the wall
pictures of every motorcycle, car, truck:
in his rusted out Impala convertible
wearing his cap and gown
waving
in his yellow Barracuda
with a girl leaning into him
waving
on his Honda 350
waving
on his Honda 750 with the boys
holding a beer
waving
in his first rig
wearing a baseball hat backwards
waving
in his Mercury Montego
getting married
waving
in his black LTD
trying to sell real estate
waving
back to driving trucks
a shiny new rig
waving
on his Harley Sportster
with his wife on the back
waving
his son in a car seat
with his own steering wheel
my brother leaning over him
in an old Ford pickup
and they are
waving

holding a wrench a rag
a hose a shammy
waving.

My brother helmetless
rides off on his Harley
waving
my brother's feet
rarely touch the ground—
waving waving
face pressed to the wind
no camera to save him.

Elegy for Muncey

"Anything less than death is a minor accident."
Bill Muncey

Skimming your boat
over choppy Detroit
River always
the favorite
we stood on the banks
shirts off drunk
yelling garbage
floating by
boats roaring
spitting up spray
the closest thing
to angels I ever saw
in Detroit fast and loud
death dancing on water
you died racing far
from these chilly waters
you blessed each summer
your boat in the lead
coming around
the Roostertail turn
Muncey, Muncey
a pure word rising
your survival
the only accident
we believed in.

March 17, 1972

I stood for a long time
watching lights smear the wet street.
My feet planted themselves in mud.
Police radios squawked against each other.

The pint in one pocket
tugged down my jacket.
I felt its weight
cold in my hands.

Ambulances took away two injured,
one dead. Friends. Five men pushed
the crushed car back on its wheels.
A wrecker hauled it away.

Show's over, boy, a cop said.
I yanked my feet out and turned
away. I can tell you this
years later. You've probably
been there:

on Alvina, the sharp curve
by the Dairy Queen, the stump
next to the ditch.
An older brother's i.d.
Someone's father's car.

Maybe you walked home
a different way. Maybe
you didn't stop to sit
on a swing behind the grade school.
Maybe the rain stopped
on your night.

Me, I banged myself
against a cyclone fence.
I finished my bottle
and fingered old stitches.
I wouldn't be smart again
for years.

Real Dancing

"It's only in bars like this that people do real dancing."

Tonight a broken family sweeps the floor,
mama out there stepping down
with her right foot, jerking
her ass that way, short step right,
ass jerk.

Her son, the blond kid
with matted hair hanging in his eyes
jumps up and down off the cement floor
celebrating the empty space.

His fat sister rolls back and forth.
She can't jump up or bend down
but oh she sways
that woman inside her doing leaps
and spins.

On the other side of the bar
a pale, skinny guy in black,
chain holding his wallet to belt,
waves his stringy hair
looks like a knife ready to dance
into a soft belly.

He dances with a woman, his twin
except for the small mounds
bouncing loose under her shirt.
They stomp the floor
like they're trying to keep something down
that could swell up
and stop the music.

All these bodies
dance in aisles, between tables,

the jukebox punching out
song after song.
Even the ugly drunk
who's been sitting at the bar since noon
steps around them
on his way to the pisser.

Ted's Bar and Grill

for Russell Rock

Every night at this place
with one pool table, one pinball machine
we shuffle our greasy boots
up to the bar where Jeannie serves up drinks
with her long blond hair and nice ass.
She's engaged to "a good guy—
he don't hang out in bars"
and she don't have no trouble handling the drunks
because she's so sweet even the drunkest pigs
get shamed by her blushes.

And there's this retarded guy Herbert
with a screwed up face
who can't talk right and drools a lot.
He's always trying to pick up Fat Mary
who needs two bar stools, one for each cheek.
She's always telling him
that she'll bring her boyfriend in
and every time she does
he puts on his sad dog face and starts to moan.
Nobody can stand the noise
so we end up dragging him out the door.
We all know Mary ain't got no boyfriend
and she's lonely as hell
and we're all waiting for the night
she'll get drunk enough so Herbert don't seem retarded
and take him home with her.

Then there's Marty
who just about owns the pool table—
nobody can beat him and no one will play him
but he won't go nowhere else to play.
And old Ted the owner
he just raised prices again and we're pissed

but it's hard to bitch at Jeannie
and Ted hardly comes around anymore
except to kick us out and close up.

Not much excitement here—
not since Jerry kicked the shit out of his boy
when he came in all high on dope
to try and borrow his old man's car.
That was some fight—but a drinker always beats a doper,
everybody knows that.

When the bar closes, I drift on home
and go to bed. Some days I feel
real stupid about myself and my drinking
and can't fall asleep.
I think about going in to work
with a head on again.

I got to stop hanging out at Ted's.
Some nights I try to stay home after work
but then I start thinking
that maybe I'll miss something—
that maybe somebody will beat Marty
or pick up Jeannie or kick Ted's ass
or maybe Herbert will really pick up Mary
walk out the door holding her hand
looking back at me with his goofy face
finally smiling
and twisting my own sour mouth
into a grin.

Hard Times in the Motor City

When Louie got married
somebody gave him
a broken bicycle for a present
in all sad seriousness.

Louie gave it back—
him and his new wife
traveling light—
a toaster and clock radio
heading south west east
wherever jobs might be.

■

Up and down the streets
men mow their lawns
do yardwork
many try to grow vegetables.

Some of the wives work now
behind counters at McDonald's
marking clothes at K-Mart
pulling in minimum wage
grocery money for another week.

Everybody's already had a garage sale.

■

In the bar
Steve talks about
the afternoon tv movie
about Elvis
about fighting
anyone.

He says he'll dig ditches
or clean shitholes
all he wants is a job.
He's got a wife, two kids.
He looks me hard in the eye:
"a man can always afford a drink."

■

Dennis, laid-off trucker
borrowed some money
took his rig to Florida
loaded up a truck full of pot
sells it out of his basement
to help make house payments.

Dennis sits on his porch
smoking up the profits
singing old rock and roll songs
his electric guitar plugged into the bushes.

■

An old man talks about the Great Depression:
"you don't see nobody jumpin' out of windows
around here."

But in the backyards of Detroit
Warren, Hazel Park, Center Line
men on their knees
pray over
their rotten tomatoes
their deformed carrots
their ragged, ragged lettuce.

5000 Apply for 100 Jobs

I stood in line, drunk with the cold
shuffling toward the factory door.
Hundreds danced slowly in front of me,
hundreds behind. Some of us I knew were poor
with pink skin sticking out
of what we wore.
When the man said *go home, that's it,*
some kicked the ground and swore.
Others moved on quickly
having been here before.
At least I have another job—minimum wage—
washing windows, sweeping floors,
so I felt a bit of joy inside that big sadness,
like Happy Hour at the Goodwill Store.

No Job

Laying off, they're laying off
softball teams swinging
their bats suddenly heavy
the ball so small.

A ton of robots in his dream
march across the field
men nervously put
out their cigars.

Tire tracks across his lawn
faded stripes, dead tiger
old soldier not sure
about the war, any war.

He drinks Mad Dog
he smokes homegrown
he sits naked with the want ads
he barks up the wrong tree.

He wants to skin himself
hang his hide out to dry
bugs, sticky dimes crawling on his arms
there's no jobs, no no no jobs.

He burns a cigarette
into the arm of his chair
his oldest child
his father, the sofa.

A woman shrinks his house
with a vacuum cleaner.
It's his wife
she sucks him up.

He sells his car, buys a junker
he sells his records, has a yard sale
he gets rid of his dog: tiny hairs
he'll never be gone.

Around the block he walks, sun
drying him out. Neighbors
his age, younger, older: raisins.
They nod, no jobs.

High school, toking behind auto shop
parking lot sticky in the heat.
Ford, Chevy, Chrysler—
where you gonna work?

Sweat darkens his shirt. He walks
home, drains a beer, sucking something
down at last. His father got him in: greasy
coveralls. Nice check. Car. Wife. House.

She cooks mac and cheese
she cooks dented cans
he goes for long walks
he never gets lost.

He pulls out
all the bushes in his yard
swinging a shovel at the roots.
He chases the paperboy.

Television smashed in the driveway.
His wife hides with neighbors.
No, no, no jobs:
he throws his knife in the air.

Still Lives in Detroit: #1, Rome Street

Chalk runs like mascara
over the pitted cement
fades in the rain:
Cindee is a Hore.
Who is a whore tonight?
This cement gives back nothing.
Scars on her knees as she reads it.

Mitch Ryder screams from a car radio
a razor cutting through
the night's wet skin.
A kid slumps against the door
smoke rising out the window.
He spits into the rain.

Across the street a car rusts.
On blocks. For years.

#2, Parking Lot, Ford Sterling Plant

Empty pallets stacked against the fence,
a few cars scattered across the blacktop,
a barren landscape decaying under grey sky.

167 days since the last work-loss accident
This lot under closed-circuit surveillance
Authorized personnel only

An empty bag blown flush against the fence.
A set of keys in the middle of an aisle.
A flattened oil can, a lottery ticket,
a paperback with no cover.

There's a man in this picture.
No one can find him.

#3, Behind Chatham's Supermarket

In the alley behind Chatham's
two boys and an older man stand stained
in aprons, lean against the dumpster smell.

In the field between Chatham's and Delta Drugs
broken glass, candy wrappers, footprints
lie frozen in earth.

Three cigarettes smoke the air.
Across the street, the high school
spills toward them.

The boys pose in faded letter jackets,
playing hooky briefly again, stamp
guns on their belts.

The man is smiling as one boy speaks.
He is watching the back door, measuring distances.
No clues to what has put him here.

If I could, I would watch until the earth thawed,
took in new shapes, shifted with possibility.
What could be a rat moves through the picture.

Snowstorm in Detroit

A stuck car bleeds
transmission fluid, spots the new snow.

Across the street, a car pulls
to the curb. The woman who was stabbed
last week struggles out, eases
up her steps.

The morning paperboy, hours late
runs down the street
tripping on his unbuckled boots
dropping his papers.
He gets up, walks away
the wet papers blowing in the snow.

An old pickup skids
into a parked car, keeps on going.
A man in a t-shirt running,
yelling, throws snowballs.

The guy who once set a cat on fire
pushes himself down the street
leans into the storm.

Next door, a child cries, a woman cries,
a dog barks and scratches the door.

The stuck car dies.
The preacher gets out, slams the door
stands in the street
hugging an armload of prayers.

The Man Stuck between His Shoes

takes a long drink of thunder, lightning, rain
personified as a bird, personified as a car
personified as a wine, liquid bird going down
drinks the stubble of his beard, his body's smell
spreading around him, a blanket no one would trade for
the broken glass he drinks down, the steel cages
of the stores, drinks down the suspicion of eyes
the faces chewing dumpster meals, drinks down
the spaces between houses, the rubble, the empty
windows, the snow dressing what survives, the spreading
disappearance of the East Side, oh, he drinks it all
down, the man holding a knife to his mother's throat
Christmas Eve, the son killing his father, yes, right now
with a baseball bat, the young ones shooting before
they shave, bored with disease, the angry dust
of alleys where no one calls for rags, the hollow
churches turned to missions, the alcoholic ward called
street called bench called crime, the drug ward called
alley called gun called night, and night in day
and he swallows, swallows all till thunder, lightning
rain rise from his throat
no thunderbird, no phoenix.

Watching My Old House Burn on the News

A sixty-second spot:
another abandoned house
torched in Detroit,
a slow day for news.

Water shoots from the hoses,
mixes with a light rain.
A bunch of kids stand nearby
mugging for the camera.

No bodies to carry out, nothing
to save. The firemen
keep it from spreading.
My mother cries.

On the sheets of a tired bed
in the upper flat of that house
I was conceived
on a wet night like this,

September, rain knocking
leaves from the trees,
two babies crying
in the other room.

My mother's tears fall tonight
not like that rain at all
not like those falling leaves.
Like those flames. Like that fire.

Moving My Grandfather

He wouldn't move
after fifty years in the same house.
He put a burglar alarm sign on his door
a chewed-up shoe in his yard
a baseball bat by the door
though he had no alarm, dog, strength.

He didn't carry a wallet.
Pinned money to his shirt
but had no sign for that.
He got jumped often
for change not worth
kicking an old man's ass for.

Last time they cracked his skull
blood in his white hair.
He came out of the hospital
lobotomized by fear
sitting in his front room
listening to the street.

We packed up his belongings
three broken tvs
a stringless harp from the burned-out
church across the street.
My father cried its music
up and down the stairs.

We loaded up fast, in daylight
one truckload. No one could figure out
how to free the rocking chair
chained to the porch
so we left it
creaking in the heavy air.

TWO

Digger Drives to Work

The morning paperboy
tire groaning against fender
the grass plastic with frost.
A car backs out of a driveway.
A car backs out of a driveway.
A car backs out of a driveway.
Gates close.
Dogs out.
From fence to fence to fence
the same dog's face,
steamy breath
rising through the mesh.

■

In the rear-view mirror
the same grim face
in the car behind you
puffing a cigarette
looking at a watch.
You check yours.
You will be on time
again.

■

An accident on the expressway.
You crawl past
the flashing lights,
bitch about the tie-up.
A policeman waves you past.
You nod your head
moving with the flow until
you see a shoe on the ground.
A corpse with one shoe.

You look at your feet
on the pedals
for a half second:
work shoes.
Check watch.
Your heart stutters.

The song changes
and you nod your head again.
But the sirens.
Suddenly you notice
the sirens
and turn up the radio.

■

Your car speeds up as traffic thins.
You look at your watch.
Maybe you will be late after all.
With one hand you open
your cold black lunch bucket:
salami again.
You lick the mustard off your fingers.

Digger Goes Hunting

When fall starts chilling into winter
you pack up your rifle and drive north
with a couple buddies from the plant.

You stagger through the woods
whiskey heavy
and whiskey warm
startling every animal for miles
with your song.
You doze off against a tree.

When you wake up
a big animal is moving toward
you through the trees.
You pull your rifle to your shoulder
and shoot twice.
The animal falls.

You stand over
a young doe.
You don't have a permit
so you get a shovel
bury it
chipping at the hard earth
sweating whiskey.

The next day
padding sober down a trail
you feel that doe's heart
beating under your feet.
Tree branches fill your head
and you suddenly fear everything
alive and moving in these woods.

You clutch your gun tighter
and move on.
You have trusted steel too long
to stop now.

Digger's Thanksgiving

You invite your parents over
because your mother can't do
turkeys anymore.

Your mother asks you
if you're still at Ford's
three times in ten minutes.
Your father talks on and on
about the football game on tv.
Your son hides in his room.

During dinner your mother repeats
"everything is so delicious,
so delicious," over and over.
You're hungover
and barely touch your plate.

They leave after pie
to get home by dark.
As your mother steps out the door
"everything is so delicious"
she falls and breaks an ankle.

In the hospital waiting room
you think of your parents
still living in the city
though they've both been mugged.
You want them to move to the suburbs
but they refuse.

They're like tired flies, you think,
they barely move at all.
Just waiting for someone to kill them.
You try to think of something you could do.

You think of putting them in a home.
You remember as a child
pulling the wings off of flies:
so delicious, so delicious.

Digger Shovels the Snow

After dinner you trudge
out in your green boots
and ragged army coat
dragging the shovel behind you.

Up and down the street
men scrape shovels against cement
lift them up full of snow
and dump them onto their lawns.
You stand tall for a moment
then bend down
and join them.

The sky darkens into night
while you shovel and lift
the wet shining snow,
clearing the driveway and sidewalk,
dividing your yard into rectangles,
fitting into the grand design
of the street.

Your daughters roll around in the yard
making angels in the snow,
their faces red and wet.
You bend down again
for that heart attack
you know will kill you.

Digger Has a Dream

You lie in a parking lot
groaning like a car
that won't start
rolling over and back
over and back.
A woman with jumper cables
dangling from her steel breasts
clamps your hands
and you jerk to a start
rolling off down the road.
The cables seem to run on forever
your wife and kids
grow out of your legs
all attached, rolling along
until the cords jerk you to a stop
yank you back to the woman
then away then back
then away then back.
You wear away the asphalt
making chuckholes with your elbows
and you roll and roll
and you want to rip the cables
off your arms
but you're afraid
you might never move again.

You see other people dancing around you
skipping over your rolling bodies
and speaking silver coins
which fall in front of you
but the cables hold your arms
tight to your sides
and you roll right over them.

Tar fills your eyes and mouth
and you cannot see your family anymore
as you head for the one big chuckhole
that could swallow you all.

Your wife shakes you awake.
For one long moment
you cannot lift your arms.
You lie in bed and shake
remembering the safety posters in the plant:
Daydreams Can Cause Nightmares.
You grind your fists into your eyes
and think about
the daydreams to come.

Digger Waters His Lawn

You drink beer after beer
on your porch staring
at your sun-scorched lawn
on your first weekend off
in two months.
Your neighbors' lawn mowers growl
at you from all directions.
If it don't grow
then I don't have to cut it,
you think, but lift yourself
at last out of the broken rungs
of your chair and move
toward the side of the house.
You unweave the hose tangled
from the girls' water fight
like it's a rope on a ship—
you are in a late movie you saw last week—
you are on the ocean and this rope
anchors you down.
Suddenly the hose unkinks
and squirts you in the face.
It is not salt water,
not fresh.

You stand in the driveway
watering the lawn, garden
the side of the house
holding the limp hose,
pissing on everything.

Digger Can't Sleep

You've been in and out of bed
three or four times already.
Tires squeal around the corner
as you click off the tv
interrupting the national anthem.
You step onto the porch
as two cars pass under the streetlight
playing cat and mouse.
A cool breeze sneaks up your boxer shorts.
The lights are out in all the windows
up and down the street
the only noise
those screaming cars.

You remember
when you were a screamer
on your Harley
that fast breathing roaring
through cool mornings like this
not even drunk
just wild with speed and noise
that wind blasting your body
sometimes
parking at the corner
sneaking down to your girl's house
knocking on her window
pulling her out onto the damp grass.

In the morning it will be coffee
and the long bumpy drive.
You think of the fork lifts at work
and their hot gassy breath
grunting up and down the greasy aisles.
You think of your wife's thick white thighs.

You suck in this cool night air
holding your breath
holding your shorts open
taking it all in.

Digger Arrives Home From Work

A girl skips down the street.
The dogs watch.
Beware of dog.
Beware of dog.

You swing your car
into the driveway.
The afternoon paperboy
is fighting on the front lawn
with your son.

You want to pull out
drive right past
pull into another driveway.
You think whose wife
you'd want the most.
But you know it would be
just the same.

Your son is winning the fight.
You take some satisfaction
before you belt him
kick him in the house.

You take the paper
from the boy
whose mouth dribbles blood:
"tough luck kid."

You bump into his bike
and it falls over.
He spits blood,
"I'm collecting today."
You give him an extra dollar.

■

Your son's stereo jolts the air.
You turn it down.
"What was that all about?"
He stares at the cracked window.
You want to hit him again.

You grab a beer from the fridge
yell at your wife.
You wander off into the living room
turn off the television
recline in your reclining chair
open up the paper.
Your eyes on the ceiling.
Faded paint.
You fade,
newspaper over your eyes.
The smell of newsprint
and blood.

Digger Goes on Vacation

The maps from AAA, the tourbooks,
you are well-prepared:
Florida here we come.
For the first time
your son will not go with you.
He has a legitimate excuse:
a job at the corner store.
It is only you and the girls.
You think of your wife
as a girl.
You think
that you have given her nothing.
At the first Stuckey's on the road
you buy her a box of peanut brittle
and smile weakly
as she kisses your cheek.
Then you think of the plant
she is kissing you good-bye
in the morning.
You feel a chill
maybe wind on your neck.
You have two weeks.
Your body shakes
as you pull back on the road:
you have fifteen more years.

■

First night
you stop at a motel
off of I-75 in Kentucky.
At a diner
you eat a late dinner
the girls nodding off to sleep
in their hamburgers.

You look at your wife.
If somehow she could lose some weight.
Then you look at your belly
hanging over your belt:
but mine's hard, you tell yourself,
muscle.

You punch your gut:
*if we could just lose
all this weight.*

"Digger?"
"Oh . . . yeah."
You pay the bill
and walk across the street
to the motel
squeezing your wife's hand
like a snowball
you want to melt.

■

You lie in the sand
the sun crisp on your back.
You will get burned.
You always do.
You try to read a book
in the bright glare—
the same book you brought
on vacation last year:
The Godfather.
At a cabin in Northern Michigan
you read 150 pages
and killed mosquitoes.

She packed it to keep me busy,
keep my eyes off the women.

You look over at your wife
wearing a floppy sun hat and bulging out
from her bathing suit.
You throw sand on her belly:
"hey Loretta, gimme a beer."
She hands you one
from the cooler by her side.

She really does
care about me,
you think, and suddenly
you are happy and smile.
You put the cold beer
against her neck
and she jumps up screaming.
"Hey baby, I love you."
"What?"
She takes off her sunglasses
and smiles, hugging you.
"You haven't said that since . . .
last year's vacation!"

You stare out at the sea of skin
and wonder when
you'll say it again.

■

At the beach
your foot in the sand
outlines the part
you weld onto axles.

"What's that, Daddy?"
You kick sand
over the drawing,
"Nothin'."
But no matter how many times
you kick the sand
it still looks like
something.

■

In a motel in Tennessee
you peel off your skin
to gross your daughters out.
"Oh Daddy, that's sick!"
You laugh
and rub your vacation beard:
"when all this skin is gone
I'll be a new person."
"Who will you be then, Daddy?"
"I'll be an astronaut.
So I could get lost in space."
"You're already lost in space,"
your wife shouts from the bathroom.

That night after dinner
you drink alone
at a local bar.
Your hands hold up your head
like obedient stilts.
This is how you always
become a new person.
You talk to the bartender:
"I used to be an astronaut."
And he believes you.

Digger's Daughter's First Date

You wait up with your wife,
shifting together in the silence.

When she comes home
exactly at twelve
the car idles too long in the driveway
before she gets out.
But that's a good sign, you think,
that means they didn't park before.

When she walks in the door
you shove your cigarette butt
in the wrong beer can.
You groan—*that's why I got married*—
a butt in the wrong can.

Her cheeks shine
like a clean ashtray.
You smile.

Digger Gets a Dog

Your brother's dog has puppies
and you decide the family
needs a dog.
Your wife makes faces.
But your daughters shout their support
and your son looks interested.

You bring it home one night
while your wife is shopping
and watch it piss on the rug.
The kids fight—no one
will clean it up.
You devise a system to take turns,
make a chart, tape it to the fridge:
everyone must have responsibility.

The next night at dinner
you decide it's time to name the dog.
Your wife and daughters
want to name him King.
Trying to dethrone me, you think
and suggest Clint.
"Clint's not a dog's name."
"Clint, yuk."

You won't give in.
Your stomach churns
as you slurp your jello.
"Clint, and that's final."
You smile as your wife rubs
her forehead and the girls run off
crying, slamming doors.

You look at your son.
He gives you a smirk
and a closed-fist salute:
"Clint, yeah."
You get up and take the dog on the porch.
You look through the screen at your son
and hold the dog
tight to your chest: *at last*
we've agreed on something.

Digger Thinks about Numbers

You look at the number
above the freeway to see
how many cars have been made
in America this year.
The car drifts
and you swerve back
into your lane.
Each time you have to look.

■

Every day you're supposed to make
800 axle housing tubes.
If you make 800
you sit down for the rest of the day.
Some days you try to make it
and do. Some days you try
but the machine breaks down.
Some days you break down.

And every day you start back at zero
like you never made those parts
the day before.

You want them to put a sign over the freeway:
"Digger made 160,000 parts so far this year."
You want your neighbor to come over
and congratulate you. But
he ties brake cables—he'd want a sign too.

■

Your wife hits your arm:
"What are you trying to do, get us killed?"

You think of the sign at the police station:
auto injuries ———
fatalities ———.
You grab the wheel and hunch over,
guarding the only life
you're ever going to have.

Digger Laid Off

Tonight you beat up four little kids
to get a baseball at Tiger Stadium.
After the game you sit in a bar
watching fat naked women
rub mud over their bodies.
You throw your ball in the mud pit
and a dancer picks it up
rubs it over her muddy crotch
and throws it back to you.
In the parking lot
you throw the ball against a windshield
but it will not crack.

THREE

First Job

My mother paid me a nickel
for each cricket I caught.
Looking down the stairs,
nursing my baby sister,
she wanted them silent, dead.
My brother sulked, wanting
to trap, release.

I hunted by sound, stalking them
among old newspapers, broken toys,
trapping them under a cup.
I showed each one to my mother
who sat on the sagging couch upstairs
burping the baby.

Dangling in air, they spit
on my hands as I dropped them
in the toilet, watched them dance
on the surface, swirl away.

I sat in the cool, damp basement
and listened to the silence
of a job well done.
I rubbed the coins together
and made a sweet sound.
I rubbed and rubbed
but no one came.

A Good Customer

Stanley came in every day
for two bottles of white port, $1.05 each
and I sold it to him, paper bags full
of what I knew was death.

His liver: the sweat
on his forehead bled down
cheeks full of poison and pain.
His skin was so doughy I wanted
to believe I could squeeze his body together
into someone who wouldn't need this.

His face filled with a sadness
I had never known, getting my kicks
off a few beers on weekends.
Some days, I took longer to wait on him.
I believe now it was not to cause him pain.
I watched him scratch with his old claws,
dancing the slowest dance I ever saw.

In ten years, I've emptied a few bottles.
I've never seen his face in one of them.
Maybe he still waits in line somewhere
his whiskers turning into specks of death.

He was the first person
I ever wanted to die.

Hold Up

Saturday around six
a man with a gun
asked for all the money.
I filled a paper bag,
change ringing over tile.

Lay down, he said.
Don't get up, he said.
I lay there hugging the floor
as if it could save me.
This part sits deep in my gut:

cold steel against my temple.
Don't move, he said. And I felt
a strange calmness then,
like my body was already
falling through the floor.

Don't move, he said again,
softly, as if sharing a confidence.
And I nodded then
to assure him his secret
was safe with me.

He stepped over me and out the door.

When the operator asked
if it was an emergency
I did not know.

Red lights circled in
through the windows and sharp voices
scratched the hot night air.

I could not tell, then or now
what he wore, how tall,
what build

though some nights I hear his voice.
Always, I'm in bed, watching the moon swell
or touching the woman sleeping beside me.

The voice says *lay down.*
I fold my hands behind me.
I close my eyes and arch my back.

It was a Saturday night
around six. There was
a man with a gun.

The voice says *don't move.*

Short-order Cook

An average joe comes in
and orders thirty cheeseburgers and thirty fries.

I wait for him to pay before I start cooking.
He pays.
He ain't no average joe.

The grill is just big enough for ten rows of three.
I slap the burgers down
throw two buckets of fries in the deep frier
and they pop pop spit spit . . .
psss . . .
The counter girls laugh.
I concentrate.
It is the crucial point—
they are ready for the cheese:
my fingers shake as I tear off slices
toss them on the burgers/fries done/dump/
refill buckets/burgers ready/flip into buns/
beat that melting cheese/wrap burgers in plastic/
into paper bags/fries done/dump/fill thirty bags/
bring them to the counter/wipe sweat on sleeve
and smile at the counter girls.
I puff my chest out and bellow:
"Thirty cheeseburgers, thirty fries!"
They look at me funny.
I grab a handful of ice, toss it in my mouth
do a little dance and walk back to the grill.
Pressure, responsibility, success,
thirty cheeseburgers, thirty fries.

May's Poem

"I want to write a poem
about something beautiful,"
I tell May, the cook.
On my break from the grill
I stand against the open kitchen door
getting stoned.

"That shit make you stupid."
May wrinkles her forehead
in waves of disapproval.

"I don't need to be smart
to work here."
The grease sticks to my skin
a slimy reminder
of what my future holds.

"I thought you was gonna be
a writer. What about that
beautiful poem?"

I take a long hit
and pinch out the joint.
"You'll end up no good
like my boy Gerald."

"May, I'm gonna make you
a beautiful poem," I say
and I turn and grab her
and hug her to me
pick her up
and twirl her in circles
our sweaty uniforms sticking
together, her large breasts

heaving in my face
as she laughs and laughs
and the waitresses all come back
and the dishwasher who never smiles
makes a noise that could be
half a laugh.

But she's heavy
and I have to put her down.
The manager stands there:
"Play time's over. Break's over."
Everyone walks away
goes back to work.

This isn't my beautiful poem, I know.
My poem would have no manager
no end to breaks.
My poem would have made her lighter.
My poem would have never put her down.

Mops

I've had five jobs
where I had to mop,
each mop the obvious
same woman's hair.

I cannot tell you
I have loved that woman,
that I wanted to give back
her hair clean and golden.

Everything turns water black.
Pouring it down whatever hole
was used for pouring, I watched
like a lifeguard, for trouble,
for anything to save.

Twist and squeeze gave me
most pleasure, priest purging sin,
the constant confession
of dirty water. Though never enough

pleasure, never enough broken glass
to fill my pockets.
I never believed
it was as hard an absolution.

To clean was never noble.
The bending down, following
pointed fingers to, not sin, but blood,
glass, hot fudge, grease, lawyer's piss.
The only god I prayed to
was one who improved grip, aim.

It was a job, to clean.
The pay was bad, still is.
I had a broom too
but it tells the same story.

Places Everyone

"There's a place for everyone in our organization."

The best-looking women
work in bedding.
The fat, wholesome women who smell like cookies
work in kitchen.
In china and silver
the women are fragile, elegant, middle-aged.
In men's
hen-pecked grandfathers
with their pasty smiles
suck ass to sell suits.
The healthy bastards
with sons who have failed them
work in sporting goods.
All the angry people
work downstairs in the stockroom
heaving boxes in and out of trucks.
That's where all the blacks work.
I work down there
tossing boxes with them
not even trying
to match their anger.

For People Who Can't Open Their Hoods

Some fat lady in a mink
storms in
says her car won't start
left her lights on
got her son outside with cables
but they don't know how
to open the hood.

Because I'm head stockboy
because she's a good customer
they send me out to help her.
I grin at the two of them
son fat as mother
shaking pink cheeks in the cold
cables dangling from his gloved hands.
He hands them to me
like they're dead snakes.

I pop open the hood
of the mother's new Grand Prix.
They stand aside yapping
not even looking at me.
I start up the son's Cadillac
and sit behind the wheel for a while.
They look at the mother's packages
that I carried out minutes before
without getting a tip.

I rev it up, my foot to the floor
while I check out the plush interior
stereo tape deck, digital clock, cruise control
power everything.
I beep the horn.
They stand in the cold
suddenly looking at me.

I put the car in reverse
and back out to move in position
for the jump.
I put it in drive and grip the wheel
and for one long moment
they think   I think
I will drive away.

The Rubber Finger

has a softly rounded rubber tip
and six air holes which form an arrow
shooting forward. Its rounded grooves
soon wear down from strenuous use.

The fingers come in different sizes.
I wear a twelve, the biggest available.
The women bookkeepers snicker
"Size twelve, eh?"
They stare at my crotch.

Every day I sit at my desk
flipping through accounts with my size twelve
those checks never knowing
what hit them.

Recycled Lunchbucket

I wiped it clean, sprayed black paint
over the farm animals, the barn.

Then it looked like the others in the factory:
small, black houses, our little coffins.

Mornings, I made its bed: baloney and cheese,
a mealy apple, old heart.

Slow death in plastic: melted cheese, sour meat.
I swallowed all evidence.

At night it banged its emptiness against my leg.
I gripped it like a paid stranger.

This went on for months. Here and there
chipped paint—the raised cloth—animal parts:

a pig's face, horse's tail, hen's wing
peeked through their nightmare of a barn

until I slaughtered them all again.

Factory Jungle

Right after the seven o'clock break
the ropes start shining down,
thin light through the factory windows,
the sun on its way to the time clock.
My veins fill with welding flux—
I get that itchy feeling I don't belong here.

I stand behind the biggest press in the plant
waiting for the parts to drop down into the rack,
thinking about what that mad elephant
could do to a hand.

I'd like to climb one of those ropes of light
swing around the plant
between presses, welders, assembly lines
past the man working the overhead crane
everyone looking up, swearing off booze, pills,
whatever they think made them see me.
I'd shed my boots, coveralls, safety glasses, ear plugs,
and fly out the plant gate
past the guard post
and into the last hour of twilight.

The parts are backing up
but I don't care.
I rip open my coveralls and pound my chest
trying to raise my voice
above the roar of the machines
yelling louder than Tarzan ever had to.

Pee Wee

Pee Wee has that automatic smile
for anyone he sees,
that smile, no teeth, just gums, lips,
pillows of flesh.

Pee Wee fits in coveralls
like a kid in a clown costume,
the material blossoming out loose
over his tiny bones.

Pee Wee's been here 29 years.
He smiles that smile.
He looks through glassy eyes.
He pops pills every day.

Pee Wee has an easy job,
painting lock-tite on axle-housing welds
as they ride by on hooks.
He cranes his long neck around the housings
looking for the foreman
then, after letting a few pass by
he grabs one he likes,
light and graceful,
his neck resting on the warm steel,
and dances the stiff housing
toward the paint house at the end of the line,
that black spraying he calls death.

Anita, A New Hire on the Line

The first time I saw you
I wondered how you could sweat
and still be so fine.

You talk about all the young dudes
after your ass,
blind to the difference
between high school and the factory.

The older women don't bother
to raise their eyes at your flirtations
your low-cut tops, your lack of a bra
on the hottest days.

Anita, treasure those breasts,
even after the rest of your body
looks and moves like ours.

Even if you're not a virgin
here your virginity is your spirit that soars
and that you haven't lost yet, laughing
loud and open-mouthed in the break room,
clomping down the greasy aisles
in your new steel-toed boots
like a kid in her father's shoes.

Anita, don't lose that spirit.
Hide it between your breasts
until you walk out the gate
then open your shirt
to the first person
with clean hands.

Work Shoes

Loaned out to another department for the day
I had a job painting the good parts green,
the bad orange.

When the line broke down
I painted my shoes green
and danced a resurrection from grease.

I was Mr. Greenshoes,
my feet so light and new
I painted my socks too.

Foreman said "Asshole,"
spit on the floor,
asked me to work late.

I said "Greenshoes don't want no overtime!"
danced for him,
followed his thumb to the door.

Getting Off Early

At a red light I strip
to the waist and stick
my head out the window.
On the radio, music
to floor it to: I make
the wind stronger.

I can feel already the shower
pounding against grease
and the lack of a woman.
Tonight, I don't want it.
I stop at the first beer store
to hold a six-pack to my forehead
and rub the sweat cool
into my eyes.

I take the first ramp down
onto the freeway and speed
toward this feeling of not stopping,
alive in this breeze, a check
in my pocket big enough
to get me through four states.
I turn up the radio and sing
my own words:
I've never been happier.
Something like that.

Factory Love

Machine, I come to you 800 times a day
like a crazy monkey lover:
in and out, in and out, in and out.

And you, you hardly ever break down,
such clean welds, such sturdy parts.
Oh how I love to oil your tips.

Machine, please come home with me tonight.
I'll scrub off all the stains on your name,
grease and graffiti.

I'm tired of being your part-time lover.
Let me carry you off
into the night on a hi-lo.

That guy on midnights,
I know he drinks,
and beats you.

Blood Flows through Steel

for my brother Tim

The first summer in the factory
we worked together, same department, same shift.
Next to each other on the line
you passing the parts to me
I got sick of seeing your greasy face.

But on breaks and at lunch
we stuck together like halves of an axle housing
welded together and painted with lock-tite.
We would have passed any water test.

When the crazy ex-p.o.w. from department 43
grabbed your balls in the john
I jumped on his back, choked till he let go.

When I burned my arm welding
your yelling and screaming
almost got us both fired.

The last day we worked together
you broke your machine
by putting in a part backwards
and I broke mine with a crowbar.
We did the factory howl all night
like happy dogs.

The next summer, on different shifts
we saw each other only at the time clocks.
You, usually drunk, and me, ready to get that way,
that one day you found my car in the parking lot
and put cold beers on the front seat
I could have kissed you with the word *brother.*

After Work

On this night of blue moon and damp grass
I lie bare-backed on the ground
and hum a children's song.
The air is cool for midnight, July.
The grass pins my sticky back.

You, moon, I bet you could
fill my cheeks with wet snow
make me forget I ever touched steel
make me forget even
that you
look like a headlight
moving toward me.

Acknowledgments

These poems previously appeared in the following publications, a few under different titles.

The Greenfield Review: "My Grandfather's Tools" and "My Mother Walks"

Passages North: "My Father Worked Late" and "Recycled Lunchbucket;" "My Father Worked Late" also appeared in the *Anthology of Magazine Verse and Yearbook of American Poetry* (Monitor Publishing, 1984).

The Harbor Review: "Wheels"

Arete: The Journal of Sport Literature: "Elegy for Muncey"

The Laurel Review: "Real Dancing"

The Texas Review: "Ted's Bar and Grill"

The Minnesota Review: "Hard Times in the Motor City" and "Digger's Thanksgiving"

The Centennial Review: "5000 Apply for 100 Jobs"

Carnegie-Mellon Magazine: "Still Lives in Detroit: #1, Rome Street" and "Watching My Old House Burn on the News"

Cutbank: "Still Lives in Detroit: #3, Behind Chatham's Supermarket"

Planet Detroit Poems!: "Snowstorm in Detroit" and "Digger Can't Sleep"

The Pulpsmith: "The Man Stuck between His Shoes"

The Louisville Review: "Moving My Grandfather"

Hiram Poetry Review: "Digger Drives to Work" and "Digger Arrives Home from Work"

The Wayne Review: "Digger Goes Hunting" and "Digger Shovels the Snow"

Green River Review: "Digger Has a Dream"

New Letters: "Digger Goes on Vacation"

"Digger's Daughter's First Date," "Digger Gets a Dog," and "Digger Thinks about Numbers" appeared originally in *Poetry East,* No. 15 (Fall, 1984).

Unrealist: "Digger Laid Off"

Three Rivers Poetry Journal, Vol. 25–26: "First Job"

Wind Literary Journal: "A Good Customer"

Poetry Now: "Short-order Cook" and "Factory Love;" "Short-order Cook" and "Work Shoes" also appeared in *Going for Coffee: Poetry on the Job* (Harbour Publishing, 1981)

The Pawn Review: "May's Poem" and "Mops"

"Places Everyone" first appeared in the *Cimarron Review* and is reprinted here with the permission of the Board of Regents for Oklahoma State University, holders of the copyright.

Sun Dog: "For People Who Can't Open Their Hoods"

event: "The Rubber Finger"

The Great Lakes Review: "Factory Jungle"

Praxis: "Pee Wee" and "Blood Flows through Steel"

The Greyledge Review: "Anita, A New Hire on the Line"

Carolina Quarterly: "Work Shoes"

SEZ: "After Work"

Some of these poems also appeared in two chapbooks, *Factory Poems* (Jack-in-the-box Press, 1979) and *On the Line* (Signpost Press, 1981).